Nonmonogamy and Sex Work

Nonmonogamy and
Sex Work

Zara Shah

**THORNAPPLE
PRESS**

Nonmonogamy and Sex Work
A More Than Two Essentials Guide

Thornapple Press, 300–722 Cormorant Street
Victoria, BC V8W 1P8 Canada press@thornapplepress.ca

Our business offices are located in the traditional, ancestral and unceded territories of the ləkʷəŋən and W̱SÁNEĆ peoples. We return a percentage of company profits to the original stewards of this land through South Island Reciprocity Trust. Thornapple Press is a brand of Talk Science to Me Communications Inc. Talk Science is a WBE Canada Certified Women Business Enterprise, a CGLCC Certified 2SLGBTQI+-owned business, and a Certified Living Wage Employer.

Cover and interior design by Jeff Werner; Substantive editing by Andrea Zanin; Copy-editing by Heather van der Hoop; Proofreading by Alison Whyte; Cover detail derived from H. Lyman Saÿen, Daughter in a Rocker (1918), public domain, courtesy Smithsonian American Art Museum.

Library and Archives Canada Cataloguing in Publication
Title: Nonmonogamy and sex work / Zara Shah.
Names: Shah, Zara, author.
Description: Series statement: More than two essentials ; 10 |
   Includes bibliographical references.
Identifiers: Canadiana (print) 20240432592 | Canadiana
   (ebook) 20240436970 | ISBN 9781990869624 (softcover) |
   ISBN 9781990869631 (EPUB)
Subjects: LCSH: Sex work. | LCSH: Sex workers. |
   LCSH: Non-monogamous relationships.
Classification: LCC HQ118 .S53 2024 | DDC 306.74—dc23

Digital print edition 1.0

To all my sex worker and nonmonogamous friends who taught me there was another way

Contents

Introduction   1

Stigma   11

   Tips for Navigating Stigma   18

   Role of Allies in Combatting Stigma   25

Intimacy   33

   Intimacy and Sex Work   34

   Intimacy, Boundaries and Relationships   43

Health   53

   Access   54

   Safer Sex Strategies   57

   Lessons   59

   The Impact of Sex Work on Mental Health   63

Notes on Solidarity   71

Final Thoughts   81

Additional Reading   85

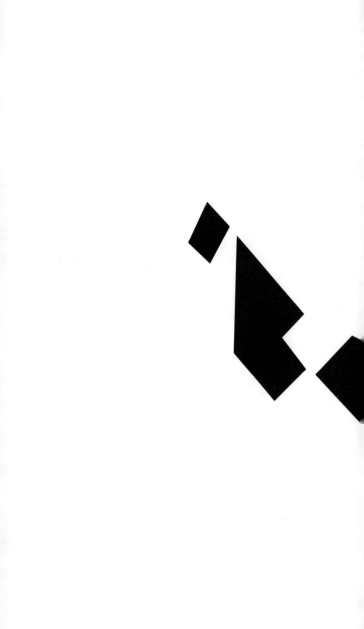

Introduction

Sex defines us in myriad ways. It's entwined with our social, cultural and political lives; our relationships; and, sometimes, our economic conditions.

But sex is more than that. As a thirtysomething woman of colour who has been involved in sex work for more than eight years, I can say that sex can also be about economic survival and the choice to reclaim some agency over our lives. I got into physical sex work through escorting for years before mostly transitioning to online sex work. My experience with sex work has been as a bisexual woman and with supports who are largely other women sex workers, though over the years I have come across sex workers of diverse genders and sexualities. I have also had the good fortune to be involved in a supportive and loving nonmonogamous relationship for roughly 10 years. Looking at my life and relationships through the combined lens of nonmonogamy and sex work has deeply influenced my values, my politics and the ways that I connect and relate to other people. This book emerged from conversations with friends and family about the intersections between sex work and nonmonogamy, as well as how these two distinct worlds can overlap and reveal a lot about those of us who do both and what we want out of our relationships and our lives more generally.

Understanding the intersections of sex work and nonmonogamy can help allies and nonmonogamous folks offer stronger support to sex workers. This understanding can also give clarity to sex workers and their partners as they navigate nonmonogamous relationships and arrive at a better place of mutual understanding and communication. These intersections include stigmas associated with both nonmonogamy and sex work, the dynamics of intimate relationships, and even how we navigate questions of sexual health. Having greater clarity about these intersections can help all of us reflect on our own ideas about nonmonogamy, sex work, and how cultural and institutional barriers can prevent sex workers and

nonmonogamous folks from accessing
the supports and services that we need.

I'd like to start by laying out some
of the more fundamental aspects of the
experience of people who work in the
sex industry. Let's first deal with the
first major objection I often hear against
the existence of sex work. Anti–sex
work individuals often form their
arguments based on the idea that sex
work is simply the last resort for women
who cannot make a living any other
way. Even though that assumption
isn't necessarily true, let's consider it
for a minute as if it were. Would sex
work be any less valid if it was, in fact,
the last resort for financially desperate
women? If this were the case for
100% of women involved in sex work,
wouldn't these workers deserve pro-
tections and rights? Wouldn't these sex
workers deserve to be free of the stigma

associated with their work? The argument that sex work is always considered out

> Even the average office worker is using their body for labour.

of desperation doesn't negate the fact that sex work is *work*.

I've had countless debates with people who, in their moralizing condescension, lament that sex workers are "selling their bodies" and should feel bad about that in some way. I'm always amused by this line of reasoning against sex work, given the realities of the world we live in. We use our bodies for labour in countless ways. The cashier or service industry worker who stands on their feet all day to help customers is also using their body for labour. The soldier who fights on battlefields and is used as a weapon also uses their body for labour. Even the average office worker is using their body for labour. Sex workers also use their bodies to provide a service: satisfying the very basic human need for sexual gratification. When critics reduce the argument to the act of "selling your body," we should critically analyze this hypocrisy by considering the impacts of misogyny and puritanical views on sex. These outdated ideas maintain rigid social institutions and norms that are at odds with people's desire for sexual agency.

Many people do not want their entire personality to be defined by their work. For the vast majority of us, work is a necessary means of economic survival. A means to an end. Some people's insistence on characterizing sex workers as lacking morality and having poor values and character speaks to the hypocrisy and misogyny of our society. People who insist on applying their moral judgments to sex workers because of what we do tend to challenge the legitimacy of sex work as labour. So even when the argument is no longer about sex workers "selling their bodies," it becomes about how only people of low character and values would consider this kind of work. I'm hopeful that this kind of oppressive thinking is slowly becoming less prevalent among Gen Z, but time will tell. For now, this moral judgment continues to be one of the many issues that sex workers consistently face, and it affects their relationships with friends and other loved ones.

I've challenged a lot of social barriers because of being a sex worker. Challenging social barriers has also been a feature of my life as someone in a nonmonogamous relationship, so I think clarifying some aspects of nonmonogamy will be helpful here.

Nonmonogamy encompasses a wide range of relationship types. For example, in open relationships, partners are free to have sexual encounters with other people outside of their relationships. Polyamory involves multiple partners who have relationships, hierarchical or otherwise, adapted to each person's comfort levels. In my own nonmonogamous relationship, I have a primary partner with whom I share a loving and honest dynamic built upon a foundation of trust and communication, which allows me to have occasional casual relationships with others without causing harm to my partner. For me, this choice was pragmatic: there was no way I could in good conscience be in a relationship without complete honesty, transparency and trust regarding my choices that could affect my partner. We began as a monogamous relationship, but after a number of months and deep conversations, we realized that nonmonogamy was a more authentic expression of the kind of relationship we wanted. That said, it's important to acknowledge that not every nonmonogamous relationship has a primary partner or central couple. Being open to and respectful of the variety and nuances of nonmonogamy will help you better explore nonmonogamous relationships and support nonmonogamous folks in your life.

For sex workers, nonmonogamy is an intrinsic part of the industry, but I'd say that the actual practice is a little more nuanced. Sex work as nonmonogamy has to be separated from nonmonogamy in personal relationships. Without establishing these sorts of boundaries, sex workers risk blurring the lines between their personal lives and work, which can result in difficulties in your relationships—trust me. I have heard from friends who do sex work that while they participate in the industry, they don't consider themselves to be nonmonogamous in their personal relationships. For many sex workers, there has to be a clear separation between their work in the industry and their personal lives.

Some important intersectional issues affect sex workers, nonmonogamous people, and those of us who fall into both categories every day. The rest of this book examines some of the most common intersections.

Stigma

"You do sex work? I can't believe you would degrade yourself like that!"
"Don't you have any respect for yourself or your partner?"

I've heard these and hundreds of other moralizing, judgmental statements over the years that aim to undermine and delegitimize not only sex workers, but also nonmonogamous relationships. When we look at the intersection between sex work and nonmonogamy, it's pretty hard to ignore the role of stigma in shaping personal and societal perceptions. People who engage in sex work or nonmonogamy—or both—are constantly made to defend themselves and their choices to others who look down on their actions and lifestyles, and who ostracize those of us who don't conform. Stigma is one of the challenges that exist at this intersection between sex work and nonmonogamy, and combatting it is an important part of supporting and standing in solidarity with both sex workers and people in nonmonogamous relationships.

So, what does stigma against sex workers look like? On the surface, it's the way that people look at you differently, treat you differently and, potentially, cut you out of their lives, all for participating in the sex industry. The moralizing and judgmental ways that people look at sex work are rooted in generations of puritanical misogyny that continues to undermine sex workers to this day. Stigma against sex workers shows up in the jokes made at our expense and the way many sex workers don't feel like they can share the details of their work with friends and family. This stigma also manifests itself in very real, structural ways. Laws that criminalize sex work give people grounds to demonize sex workers as criminals, which can make our lives hell. The stigma against sex workers trickles from the top down, reinforcing generations of assumptions, stereotypes and outright lies about the nature of sex work, who sex workers are, and what we do as an underprotected working class.

These layers of stigma intersect with similar judgmental reactions experienced by people in nonmonogamous relationships, such as being ostracized from family or isolated from friends. A whole lot of assumptions get made when someone mentions that they're nonmonogamous. Some people immediately bring up stereotypes of someone who tries to have sex with every hot person they meet. I've seen people's expressions immediately change when I mention being in a nonmonogamous relationship. Distrust. Distaste: Ugh. There's something about nonmonogamy that makes some people not only uneasy, but defensive. Defensive about the nature of their own relationships, and defensive about the institution of monogamy as a whole. Some people say that nonmonogamy is a "cop out"—a way to sleep around, to have sex with as many people as possible with no consideration for the lives of the

Sex workers and nonmonogamous people are consistently judged, on a moral basis people around us. People are often stuck in their prejudices and their presumptions about people who want different things out of their relationships. People sometimes act as though nonmonogamy attacks and undermines the very core of their own monogamous relationships. I feel like this level of defensiveness speaks both to the degree of stigma against nonmonogamy and to the level of insecurity that people have in their own relationships.

The intersecting stigmas applied to sex workers and nonmonogamous people—and those of us who are both—boil down to beliefs about sexuality and morality. Sex workers and nonmonogamous people are consistently judged, on a moral basis, as though their sexuality and sexual preferences are deviant in some way. We can chalk this judgment up to the social conditioning that results from a puritanical society that reinforces dated, moralizing and exclusionary views on sex. The common ground of experiencing social judgment and isolating behaviours is pretty consistent across both groups. As people find out you're nonmonogamous or do sex work, you can expect some of them to come at you aggressively (or defensively) about your decision. This stigma can be a pretty big barrier to finding common ground with judgmental people, meeting them halfway or having any basis for mutual understanding. Many people's minds will already be made up before even talking to you, and you may not have much luck trying to shape their opinions differently.

While there's overlap in the kinds of stigma applied to sex workers and nonmonogamous people, there are also some notable differences to consider.

While the stigma that affects nonmonogamous people can result in social impacts such as being isolated from friends, the stigma against sex workers runs deeper and has institutionalized roots. The criminalization of prostitution and the use of law enforcement to target sex workers have serious legal implications that can ruin sex workers' lives. Friends and family might have opinions and judgments about your nonmonogamous relationship, but for sex workers, others' judgments can result in being excluded and isolated from our only support networks.

It's really hard to push back against stigma directed at both sex workers and nonmonogamous people, but here are some strategies to help you navigate it.

Tips for Navigating Stigma

Part of being nonmonogamous or a sex worker is having the conviction to stay true to your beliefs and the desire to live life on your own terms, even in the face of other people's opinions about you and your choices. Having that conviction to be honest with yourself and your partners about your sexual choices will go a long way to helping you deal with the stigma you may face.

It took me a lot of reflection to become comfortable working through my own feelings about how people reacted to me being in a nonmonogamous relationship. The same may be true for you. This reflection can look like asking yourself a series of questions: Do other people's actions and words affect you? If so, why? Does their negative treatment of you come from a place of ignorance or fake concern? Asking yourself these questions and trying to come to a deeper understanding of *why* people act the way they do in judgment of you can feel liberating. In my own reflection, I also factored in my ethnic/cultural and religious upbringing when considering these questions. Factors like religion and traditional culture can absolutely affect whether family and friends object to or support your decisions, and it's important to consider these factors when trying to navigate these challenges. When you come to the realization that many people object to nonmonogamy because they approach it from a place of fear and ignorance, it helps take the power away from their words and accusations. This was especially true in my experience with some friends and loved ones who were (and still are) skeptical about nonmonogamous relationships.

Once you've reflected on and made an effort to break down the reasons for stigma against nonmonogamous relationships, you can look at methods to deal with that stigma more head-on. We can offer insights, education and carefully worded explanations to people in the hope that they will listen and change their minds. But let's be honest: Most people won't. If you have people in your life who are more open-minded and less rigid about their views on sexuality and relationships, it could be worth attempting to convince them that your decision to be nonmonogamous isn't deviant or reflective of poor morals or whatever. For those relationships that you truly value but feel are undermined by the other person's lack of education or communication about nonmonogamy, you should totally reach out and try to discuss their concerns. Sometimes, combatting stigma begins with showing them their ignorance about the topic and inviting them to consider that maybe they're missing some information that could help them see your perspective. But if someone has already made a judgment about you and your choices, they might interpret your thoughtful explanations as mere excuses for immoral behaviour.

My suggestion is this: Acceptance. Of course, it's easier said than done. Being constantly judged and mischaracterized by people can be hurtful, and that's true for everyone who's experienced having their life belittled by others. But in accepting the reality that some people will come at you for your choices, you can chip away at the kind of power these judgments can have over you. I'm not going to lie; this was one of the harder things to deal with when I felt the stigma for being in a nonmonogamous relationship. But over time, as I stopped giving any consideration or power at all to people's judgmental comments, I began to feel that weight lifting. If we feel the need to constantly validate our relationships and defend them to friends, family and even strangers, we're handing over that power to others, and it allows them to make us feel bad about our decisions. By recognizing that most people accept monogamy as the societal baseline for relationships and support it unquestioningly, you can refocus your efforts on your own relationships and your

> Constantly defending yourself requires mental effort and takes a major toll.

own happiness. Constantly defending yourself requires mental effort and takes a major toll. By not engaging with people who delegitimize your relationships, you are working to support your own values and choices about nonmonogamy.

For sex workers, navigating stigma can be more challenging. The stigma that surrounds sex work is pervasive and is articulated through more layers of society than the stigma related to being nonmonogamous. The vast social, cultural and institutional aspects of stigma against sex workers can have significant impacts on relationships, employment and housing, among other issues. Stigma that affects sex workers can lead some of us to avoid certain social situations and places where we might be treated unfairly. The stigma that limits sex workers from accessing government and social services and supports is very real and has serious consequences. If you're a sex worker navigating these challenges, it's important to consider your overall well-being. In prioritizing your well-being, you may need to be careful how open you are about sex work, such as in what capacity and to whom you talk about it. If you're unsure about the supports you might get or who may be on your side, you may need to omit certain details of your life as a sex worker in order to access services, secure housing or find employment outside sex work, or you may have to hide the nature of your work entirely. This is an unfortunate reality for many sex workers who lack the kinds of supports and allies that can allow us to be open about our work. It's an awful place to be, which is why it's so important to have

strong support networks and allies
willing to help us navigate the stigma.

Role of Allies in Combatting Stigma

There is currently a broad social
movement toward the decriminalization
of sex work, and part of that movement
involves everyday advocacy for better
treatment and respect. But this is hard
work and it's moving slowly. The
challenges resulting from stigma against
sex workers make it that much more
important to build greater solidarity
between non–sex workers (including
people who are in relationships
with sex workers) and sex workers.
Nonmonogamous folks have an
advantage in this regard because while
they experience a lot of discrimination
similar to that faced by sex workers,

they don't usually suffer the same
kinds of structural impacts because of
their choices. Specifically, the morality
that's used to judge nonmonogamous
relationships doesn't present the
same risk of ruining someone's life.
Nonmonogamous non–sex workers
can recognize the ways that they are
stigmatized and discriminated against
while extending solidarity to sex
workers and affirming their support for
a mutual effort to combat stigma. In
my experience, solidarity is key because
of how it helps create and maintain
important support networks for sex
workers. These support networks can
help mobilize people and resources
for efforts that work to champion
the rights of sex workers. The lack of
consistent support networks among
sex workers is one of the main reasons

why sex work can be so precarious
and workers are so vulnerable.

Allies can come in all forms:
romantic partners, feminists, healthcare
professionals, individuals in positions
of social power, etc. The reality is that
potential allies don't always recognize
the kind of power they have to help sex
workers in the broader effort to improve
the conditions of sex work. However,
sometimes providing that support can
come at a social cost, due to the persistent stigma of being associated with
sex workers. It might feel like being
"guilty by association," with people taking a different tone with you or instantly
judging you because you support a
friend or loved one who is involved
in the sex industry. The same kind of
vitriol that is directed at sex workers
can affect allies by extension, so it's

important for allies to have some idea of how to navigate this kind of stigma.

A few concepts can be helpful when trying to navigate stigma as someone who wants to be an ally to a sex worker, either as a romantic partner or someone wanting to show solidarity. The first is discretion. For many sex workers, being completely open about the nature of what we do is simply not an option. Because we have been forced to navigate stigma and discrimination on the basis of what we do to survive, we're often careful about who we trust with this information. In some cases, being too transparent about sex work can lead to backlash like being socially isolated, fired from other jobs or losing important support networks. So, if you're someone who has been allowed into the life of a sex worker and trusted with that information, consider the vulnerability they're demonstrating by choosing to be completely honest with you about that part of their life. Navigating the stigma is hard enough as it is, so learning how to be discreet about it in a way that's respectful, nonjudgmental and supportive is essential to being a strong ally to sex workers.

For partners of sex workers, it can be hard to know exactly how to go about supporting them and how to navigate that space where stigma and support collide. If you're a partner to a sex worker, it can be tough to see the kind of stigma and discrimination that your loved one may face. And you'll inevitably feel some degree of that stigma yourself as their romantic partner. So I feel it's important to talk about a few things that could make navigating that space a little easier. For partners of sex workers, it's crucial to communicate concerns, insecurities and any other issues before they become relationship issues. If you are prone to insecurity or jealousy, please talk about it! Talking about those issues can help you work through your feelings while strengthening communication with your partner. Talking things out in the early stages of a relationship can help you reassure one another and make you both feel more secure in the relationship. The moment you begin dating a sex worker, you'll start to more keenly feel the discrimination and stigma that they experience. You'll start to notice those subtle comments, jokes and offhand remarks that attempt to devalue sex work. Challenge those remarks, and correct people on their misinformation and prejudice. Stand with your partner and support them openly. If your partner isn't out about their sex work, communicate your support to them privately and aim to make them feel heard and understood. Every effort makes a difference in our lives, and even the smallest effort can have a big impact on us. By confronting stigma head-on as an ally, you can help change the conversation surrounding sex work and lessen some of the stigma associated with it.

Experiencing life at this intersection of sex work and nonmonogamy will always present challenges. As sex workers and nonmonogamous people, we are subjected to greater scrutiny, judged more harshly and mischaracterized more frequently. Stigma can have far-reaching consequences on the lives of sex workers, making it that much more important for allies to play a greater role in using their access

and power to support sex workers.
This could look like anything from
organizing resources with other allies
to push for community-based strategies
to support sex workers to just listening
to your partner talk about their day
as a sex worker and empathizing with
their frustrations. Whatever shape your
support takes, we feel it so deeply. I feel
so fortunate to have had meaningful
support to navigate stigma, not just with
my romantic partners but with allies
that I've made along the way who have
stood by me and other sex workers.

Intimacy

How do we navigate the more *intimate* aspects of both sex work and nonmonogamy? And what can we learn about intimacy in our personal relationships when we look at it through this lens of sex work and nonmonogamy?

I'm sure most people would agree that intimacy is a pretty important part of any personal relationship. It allows us to feel closer to someone, creating trust and a loving bond that can make us feel both vulnerable and secure. Intimacy resonates with our sense of belonging and happiness, so it really can't be overstated just how important it can be. But what happens when we connect with other people through sex work? What happens when we spend time with other people in a physically—or emotionally—intimate way that is separate from our personal relationships?

Intimacy and Sex Work

A lot of people are surprised when I tell them that intimacy is a pretty important part of sex work. And I don't mean that kind of deep intimacy that has you falling in love with the last person you had sex with, but the kind of intimacy that is subtle and reflects unique emotions that result from sex work. People assume that sex work is like a series of one-night stands or hookups, but it's really not. It's about recognizing someone's need, their loneliness and even their basic humanity. If we do sex work for an extended period of time, that kind of intimacy can affect the dynamics within our personal lives. I think it's important to get into some of these nuances so that we have a better idea of how intimacy operates within the realm of both sex work and our relationships.

When I first started doing sex work as an escort, I got an initial sense that intimacy, as I've traditionally understood it, wasn't part of the job, and neither was any sense of love or belonging. For most clients, sex is transactional. Compensation for services rendered. There's a simplicity in that dynamic that I was keen to maintain early on. But after seeing enough clients

over enough time, I began to realize
that I had oversimplified that dynamic
because I had chosen to ignore how
intimacy is expressed differently in sex
work. I started to understand that for a
small number of these clients, their reasons for seeking out a sex worker were
connected to some of these aspects of
intimacy. Some were younger men who
had a lot of problems in their romantic
lives, telling me that their personal flaws
or failures were the reason they'd been
unable to find a girlfriend or partner.
With some of them, I even got a sense
that they felt personal shame with
having "had to" see a sex worker. But I
was never offended by their expressions
of shame over "having to" seek out
my services, and I'll tell you why.

A lot of them were young men
who struggled greatly with communicating their romantic feelings, or

communicating with women, period. Their initial inability to make eye contact, their nervousness and their struggles to articulate their preferences all suggested to me that these were people who had a hard time with intimacy. The majority of my clients took a more assertive approach, greeting me with a hug and going off to look for the bed. Those few who struggled with the intimacy of the connection can give us a better idea about how we think about engaging in intimacy in sex work. I got a real sense that these clients often longed for the kind of intimacy that their friends and family were able to have in their own lives. Now, I'm not suggesting that seeing a sex worker can in any way replace the genuine intimacy that results from a meaningful relationship, but for some of these clients, it can mean the world. It allows them to feel that closeness to another human being, a sense of personal fulfillment. And a handful of these clients would share personal anecdotes or details about their lives. As a sex worker, I feel it's important to establish boundaries with clients and to not inquire or ask details about their personal lives, but when someone feels vulnerable enough to reveal those details to me, I'm not going to interfere. Some of them revealed their traumas, their personal pain and losses with someone like me, who they'd likely never see again. If this openness and vulnerability doesn't make a person question their understanding of what intimacy looks like, then I don't know what does. Those moments challenged the ideas I had previously held about intimacy and what it looks like to connect to another person. One client remarked on how our encounter had been the first time he'd been intimate with someone since his wife had passed away from cancer, and he felt grateful. That one shook me up a bit. And I'll be honest, I found myself thinking and reflecting a lot about that particular encounter. I wouldn't begin to know about how to talk about using sex as a way to cope with grief or loss, but the insights I've learned in my time as a sex worker have helped open my eyes to the complexity of intimacy.

Intimacy in sex work isn't exclusive to the bedroom, either. Online sex work has opened many avenues for sex workers who aim to provide sexual services without the need for physical contact. For most clients, the reason for seeking out a sex worker is for the basic service of sexual gratification. It's transactional. Mechanical. That's all well and good, but for others, who also

crave that deeper intimacy from sex
work, services like the girlfriend experience can tap into that sense of intimacy
with another person and can be
expressed in any number of ways.
Clients would sometimes ask if I could
create that feeling of being their girlfriend as a way to not only
create a fantasy, but also
intimacy. We could meet
up at a bar or restaurant
and have a date, go on
walks, see movies, etc. Having a
nice evening with a person, talking
about their day, holding hands and all
those little details that we sometimes
take for granted in relationships become
the core of this girlfriend experience.
Physical sex is de-emphasized so that
feelings of *intimacy* with another person
become the focus. And much in the
same way that physical sex allows

people to be vulnerable with one another, the girlfriend experience creates that sense of intimacy without the need for sex. It's the emotional connection that people crave, and that's the reason the girlfriend experience is a common service offered by sex workers. Many clients seem quite content with this dynamic, even if it's not technically real. But this service is not without complications.

Intimacy can be a powerful and satisfying connection to have with clients in sex work, but when the line between fantasy and reality becomes blurred, it can become problematic for everyone involved. Some clients become attached very quickly, and in my experience, the girlfriend experience can sometimes shift from a light and playful time to one that leaves a client feeling deeply emotionally invested and frustrated at the end of the service. In a couple of cases, clients became particularly fixated on the experience and I was compelled to end the service because I felt that the dynamic had become toxic. This is true even for a girlfriend experience provided through online sex work, which involves calls, morning texts and other cute virtual exchanges. Even an experience that is disconnected from the physical can become entirely too consuming and exhausting with some clients. I feel that this goes back to what I mentioned about people who seem insecure or deeply flustered when meeting up for sex. There's an intrinsic emotional component that makes these encounters hard for them and creates a false sense of true connection and intimacy. These experiences create the *illusion* of intimacy that is paid for and created with the consent of both parties.

But some people develop feelings, and that's only human. I've spent a lot of time thinking about whether it's fair to create that fake sense of connection to someone who might not fully appreciate the distinction between paid-for fantasy and reality. Because of those considerations, I no longer provide any kind of girlfriend experience, but it taught me so much about the longing and need that so many of us have to connect with someone else.

Intimacy, Boundaries and Relationships

When I first started reconsidering my understanding of intimacy in my sex work, I started to reflect on how it changed my outlook on intimacy within my personal relationships, too. For me, the basis of intimacy in any relationship is communication, openness and a desire to be vulnerable. It has been my experience that without these traits, relationships can get strained, cracks start to show and things eventually fall apart. And it's not because someone was a bad partner, necessarily, but there *has* to be openness for a relationship to grow and be meaningful. In my experience, relationships that didn't work out were largely because there was no genuine sense of intimacy. There was either no communication or just straight-up bad communication. Problems weren't talked about and instead left to fester and rot. All those things lead to relationship death. In my view, a strong sense of intimacy is at the core of making a relationship work in the long term.

As a sex worker, I knew the nature of my work would have an

A strong sense of intimacy is at the core of making a relationship work in the long term.

impact on all my relationships. Early in my primary relationship, I began doing sex work because it was the most accessible avenue to address my economic circumstances. Being clear with my primary partner about my sex work was absolutely essential for building a strong foundation for intimacy in our relationship. Knowing that we can talk out any concerns or fears that he has in a supportive, nonjudgmental way has gone a long way to help create trust and affirm that trust over time. With other partners, these conversations don't carry the same degree of intimacy and, therefore, are more about the practical and logistical arrangements of a relationship that is more casual. These are notable differences in how intimacy is demonstrated in a relationship, compared to in sex work. The foundation of intimacy in a relationship is trust and communication. In the case of sex work, the intimacy that is experienced is more superficial, transactional and fleeting. It's the suspension of disbelief that makes the intimacy feel real and meaningful for clients, and that's only possible if we ignore those features of intimacy in a relationship that simply don't work in the context of sex work. What we experience in a relationship with a strong foundation of intimacy is that putting *sustained* effort into being vulnerable and open to your partner is what makes a difference.

I've learned that intimacy in sex work operates in an opposite way than in personal relationships. What I mean is this: Relationship intimacy is based on trust, communication, all that good stuff. But with sex work, the intimacy is the result of something transactional, something paid for. In a relationship, you leave yourself vulnerable and open to your partner, without fear of judgment, to create trust. The intimacy is not based on money (ideally) or any type of superficial quality. In sex work, there's no investment of your time (beyond what's been agreed upon), your life or any kind of emotional sacrifice.

This contrast has helped reinforce the importance of having the qualities of true intimacy in my own relationships. The moment something as important as relationship intimacy becomes a kind of transaction, exchanging favours or compromises, it removes the trust and communication. These years as a sex worker have taught me a lot about not just sex and intimacy, but also how to better understand the differences between the two and how to better establish boundaries that I can apply to my personal nonmonogamous relationships.

When I first started getting involved in nonmonogamy, one of my main problems was the question of boundaries. I had a hard time knowing when to say yes or no, when to accommodate someone, when to prioritize my own time and well-being, and so on. This is true for most relationships, but nonmonogamous relationships can be even more complicated without boundaries. It was through my experiences in sex work that I was able to understand the importance of prioritizing boundaries in my relationships. (That said, if I had begun my nonmonogamous relationships before getting into sex work, I would likely have been able to learn things from my relationships and apply them to sex work.) In sex work, you learn to establish boundaries with clients quickly. What types of acts are acceptable versus off-limits, the logistics of any arranged date, protocols on when clients can contact you, and so on. These boundaries also extend to what types of personal questions they can ask (or that you're willing to answer), as well as limits on any number of aspects of the date to ensure your safety and everyone's enjoyment.

I used these lessons when I began navigating nonmonogamy. Establishing boundaries in your nonmonogamous relationships early on can spare you headaches, heartache and a whole lot of stress you could have done without. Whether you have a primary partner, multiple partners or any other type of nonmonogamous arrangement, laying out clear boundaries on the kind of intimacy that is expressed between couples can help you prioritize communication, transparency and trust. Unlike in sex work, though, I feel that being flexible with boundaries in relationships and discussing how each partner feels about the dynamics of various relationships is a better method than following the rigid, and necessary, boundaries we use in sex work. So much of what we do as sex workers is rooted in prioritizing our needs to ensure the safety and consistency of the work we do, but this doesn't translate as well to our personal relationships. Be flexible and aware, and think about what's best for *everyone* involved.

For me, one of the more significant draws of nonmonogamy is the realization that I don't have be limited to one romantic partner. I can share my life, and my body, with other people and have different meaningful experiences with each of them. The richness that comes from those different connections is one of most valuable parts of being nonmonogamous. And a part of that process of exploring nonmonogamy was learning to be less jealous, less self-centred, and more willing to compromise and get to know different people on different levels. These are important relationship skills that are easily transferred to the context of sex work. My ability to connect and relate well with different clients with distinctive personalities was improved by my experience with nonmonogamy. If you're a sex worker, learning from your personal relationships can give you a broader sense of how to relate and connect with potential clients. Likewise, your ability to establish boundaries as a necessary part of your work in the sex trade makes it easier to establish important boundaries in your own relationships. Navigating questions of intimacy in sex work and nonmonogamous relationships can be challenging, but it's important so that you can excel in your work and be a strong partner in your relationships.

Health

Sexual health and access to sexual health resources are some of the most important challenges that sex workers face. Depending on your city, state, province or territory, your access to sexual health resources can differ wildly, and that can pose risks to sex workers who simply don't have the means to access healthcare.

I want to break down some of these issues so that both sex workers and nonmonogamous people who

don't work in the sex trade can have
another perspective on what to expect
when it comes to sexual health.

Access

Remember the discussion about stigma
against both sex workers and nonmonogamous relationships? It's because
of that stigma that it's still hard for
sex workers to gain equitable access to
sexual healthcare across North America
and around the world. We often face
stigma on a social level, being ostracized
or insulted because we're sex workers.
But when it comes to healthcare, that
stigma becomes institutional. There are
any number of testimonials from sex
workers who have spoken out about
the discrimination they have faced when
trying to access sexual health services,

such as being outright denied or given transparent excuses. The pattern that emerges is that it's common for sex workers to face a lot of barriers in accessing healthcare. There are few jobs that are discriminated against in such plain terms as sex work. Shunned from family practices and clinics, many sex workers have been compelled to go to hospitals to receive primary care. For these reasons, it has been important for many sex workers to exercise as much discretion as possible, omitting details of their lives as sex workers from their conversations with healthcare professionals in order to access health care.

I, like lots of other sex workers, have had to be careful about who I tell, exactly, about the nature of my work. If I know that being vague about certain details about my life will allow me to have access to crucial sexual health services, I'm absolutely going to make the most of that. It's not that I *want* to be dishonest about sex work, but it's the reality of living with stigma and discrimination against us based on our chosen profession.

For nonmonogamous people, the discrimination is often less about whether or not you will get access to healthcare and more about the *kind* of care you will receive. When nonmonogamous people seek healthcare access, they are often subjected to a lot of implicit biases and stereotypes about their sexual practices. This kind of judgmental bias can affect the kinds of decisions that healthcare providers make and can undermine the patient-doctor relationship. There can also be challenges in getting more individualized care, such as more frequent sexually transmitted infection

(STI) screenings, etc. Like sex workers, a lot of nonmonogamous people might feel inclined to omit details about their sexual practices in order to access healthcare without judgment.

Safer Sex Strategies

When your well-being and livelihood are rooted in sex work, taking care of your sexual health and making sure that you are taking every possible precaution are absolutely essential. Making sure that your sexual health is impeccable gives you the freedom to go about your work without the immediate concerns that can snowball into bigger issues. Staying on top of regular STI testing, ensuring the use of condoms and other barriers, and limiting certain activities with a higher chance of STI transmission are important ways to go about taking care of your sexual health. Being open and direct about your expectations with clients is crucial because it helps you make sure that your sexual health stays in your hands. I've known sex workers who felt pressured to forgo condoms with particular clients who offered more money in exchange, but taking risks like that can absolutely backfire in the long term. STI infection and the resulting period of treatment can leave you unable to do your job for weeks, which could wreck your financial situation. Your sexual health is integral to your ability to make money as a sex worker, so taking care of it in the way you would any other essential part of your job is really important. When I was an escort, this was one of the most important realities that I quickly understood early on. As sex workers, we take on so many challenges and risks as part of our jobs. Being able to assert some kind of control and autonomy over our bodies is crucial.

Lessons

Sex work has taught me a lot about how to navigate sexual health in my nonmonogamous relationships and vice versa.

Sex work has helped me ensure that I prioritize managing sexual health risks with any potential clients. Like any job, sex work has its rules and obligations, and over the years, I've become conditioned to a certain way of thinking and a certain way of doing things. For a lot of people outside the world of sex work, STI testing or condom use may not be as consistent as they could be. For nonmonogamous people, it can be appealing to be able to have certain kinds of sex with some partners that you may not have with others. Both complacency and a desire for adventure can sometimes lead nonmonogamous people to take unwise risks. Years ago, prior to being involved in sex work, I too might have been likely to have sex without a condom or to not be as diligent with STI testing. But being in the sex trade has reminded me just how important it is to have safer sex, not just from the perspective of health, but to prioritize basic consent and respect for others. A partner or potential client doesn't consent to have a higher risk of STI infection because of my lack of care, and to not do my best  to maintain my sexual health is a huge lack of respect to the person I'm with. I would love for nonmonogamous people to learn from sex workers on this point!

Sex work has also helped me be a lot more aware of the boundaries I maintain with clients and those that I have with my romantic partners. I was surprised, at first, about how much overlap there was in my thinking about these boundaries.

Over the course of my years doing sex work, I've been able to recognize important elements of nonmonogamy that apply really well in the sex industry. On their most basic level, these elements boil down to communication about sexual health and consent. With my nonmonogamous partners, it has always been crucial to discuss the question of sexual health in a way that's direct but also respectful of the person's comfort with the dynamic between us, whether it is a more casual arrangement or one that's long term. For me, developing that habit to talk about sexual health and practices from the outset through nonmonogamy made it that much easier to bring up safer sex with clients without some of the awkwardness that can sometimes come up, especially in my early period of doing sex work.

Consent is a huge part of any relationship, but it's especially important in nonmonogamous relationships, given that there are more partners and more elements to work through. Experience dealing with consent between partners can have a clear application to sex work. Giving consent to access our bodies is a pillar of sex work, and from there, we may consent to certain acts within boundaries, such as having sex only with the use of condoms and other barriers. In both realms, a consent-based framework acknowledges the importance of establishing and following through on boundaries.

The Impact of Sex Work on Mental Health

It's my hope that the ways in which sex work has impacted my mental health over the years can potentially serve as a sort of cautionary tale for others. Getting burned out from the work is quite common throughout the industry, and is a nearly inevitable reality of doing sex work. Granted, the mental health toll that sex work can take varies widely, based on factors like the length of time you've been doing sex work and the *kinds* of sex work you do, whether physical or online. In the case of physical sex work, the mental health toll can be worse because you are in situations with more variables that can affect your safety. Anxiety can add up if you find yourself in situations where you might worry about whether or not a client will be respectful or rape you. I felt a lot of my mental health issues with physical sex work had to do with questions regarding my safety and well-being, which is what pushed me to focus more on adult content creation. Having an idea of what kinds of mental health challenges exist for sex workers can be helpful in navigating the issues around sex work.

As an online sex worker and a digital adult content creator, the degree of social media promotion required to be successful online can become exhausting, especially when we consider the reality of what it means to promote sex work on social media. Being vulnerable to social media harassment, receiving unsolicited dick pics, and dealing with the endless waves of critiques and criticisms from men about all the ways that your body could be improved can simply wear you down. And if you're from an ethnic minority like me, expect a dash of casual racism tossed in for good measure. It's for these reasons that it comes as no surprise that many adult content creators do not last longer than a few years. Between the economic competition among creators, which can get nasty, and the relentless trolling by people on social media, being a sex worker online can be *exhausting*. Vitriol is directed at sex workers on social media more often than any of us would like, but by treating it as an occupational hazard, we can minimize the emotional impact it can have on us. This can also be a situation where our partners and support systems can help alleviate some of that mental health stress. Just having someone in your life who can lend an ear and offer support or positive reinforcement can lessen the weight of mental health stress.

Because my body is the product, and it's on the internet, it's apparently fair game to critics and detractors, especially in the age of social

> To experience this kind of abuse on any persistent basis would cause significant mental health damage to anyone

media. I've been told by men to "go to the fucking gym" or to wax every strand of my body hair to satisfy their hypersexualized, idealized notions about women. I've been called a "fat Pakistani pig" by racists, and that just barely scratches the surface. To experience this kind of abuse on any persistent basis would cause significant mental health damage to anyone, and rightly so.

So, what to do? Prioritize your mental health and well-being, always. Blocking every user who leaves a toxic or inappropriate message allows it to become second nature for you, almost mechanical. It won't keep those awful comments from being sent to you, but they won't sting as much. Not engaging with trolls or people who only want to get into arguments is good all-around advice for being on the internet in 2024, but it's essential for any sex worker who wants to take care of their mental health. It's not easy to do, but it's a skill that with a great deal of practice can be honed successfully.

Sex work and taking care of your mental health means finding ways to compartmentalize your sex work life from your *actual* life. Lean into hobbies and methods of positive self-expression in your off time. Establish and stick to boundaries in your work so that you don't feel like you're always on 24/7. Taking breaks when it feels like too much is essential, and so is trusting in yourself when you feel like it's too much. Our society conditions so many of us to work ourselves to the bone, forgoing any sort of consideration of our mental well-being, and we all know the damage that can do to our lives in the long term. Sex work can be especially taxing, emotionally, psychologically and even physically. The importance of ensuring that you are making time for yourself to recuperate and take care of your well-being can't be overstated.

Every person's experience in sex work will vary. How sex workers approach health and safety can be different from person to person. The quality of and access to primary health care can be a challenge for sex workers and nonmonogamous people who still face the relentless stigma upheld by our society. Mental health issues can take a debilitating toll on us as sex workers if we don't prioritize taking care of ourselves and taking care of our emotional well-being. Since the work that we do subjects us to more stigma, discrimination and vulnerability, it's that much more important to take care of ourselves and seek out allies wherever we can to help shoulder that burden.

But mental health struggles don't just affect sex workers. Nonmonogamous people can also feel the cumulative impact of mental health stressors in similar ways. Being stigmatized because of the kind of relationships you have will almost always affect your mental health. Having to constantly justify or explain your relationship status to skeptical friends and family can be extremely draining over time. And if you're open about your relationship dynamics online, there's the potential for an onslaught of negative or sarcastic comments from trolls and strangers about your personal life. Everything is up for criticism and complaints, and it can absolutely take a toll on you. As nonmonogamous people, we can seek out support from friends and allies, help them become aware of the kind of stigma we face, and just be there for one another.

Notes on Solidarity

Solidarity. What does it look like and why does it matter?

Solidarity between sex workers and nonmonogamous people and those of us who are both means acknowledging that those of us with shared values and beliefs regarding sexuality and stigma should stand together and help one another in striving for better recognition of the challenges each group faces. It matters because as an underprotected working class, sex workers face tremendous social and institutional challenges. Nonmonogamous people also experience a lot of these social challenges, so combining efforts to establish networks of solidarity and support can go a long way toward improving the lives of people in both groups in tangible ways.

We've seen how a lot of forms of discrimination can overlap between sex workers and nonmonogamous people, and how misogyny and outdated puritanical ideals make it hard to dispel certain stereotypes. Nonmonogamous people get lumped in with people who act unethically or immorally. So how can allies offer greater solidarity with nonmonogamous people? By using and adapting some of the same strategies that can help sex workers, we can provide better support for nonmonogamous people who face discrimination.

But why does this solidarity matter? It matters because it is essential that sex workers and nonmonogamous people assert agency over their bodies, without judgment or institutional barriers. This is a huge part of the struggles of both the LGBTQ+ community and reproductive justice activists who have been working tirelessly to mobilize greater supports, and the work connects with the social movement aimed at improving conditions for sex workers. But this intersection between sex work and nonmonogamy is rooted in experiences of stigma and discrimination that are so closely linked, which makes it that much more important to stand with one another. People who have shared struggles or pain should find comfort in a support network with others with whom they can empathize and connect. Solidarity between these groups matters because we share core, fundamental values around sex positivity and a desire to live our lives free of societal judgment and barriers. But because sex workers bear the brunt of these challenges, it is that much more important for nonmonogamous folks to be aware of how this stigma and discrimination can keep us from forming these important bonds.

A big part of the discrimination against nonmonogamous people is rooted in the language that's used to undermine them. People use judgmental language or loaded words and expressions as a way to judge and unfairly characterize nonmonogamous folks. One important way to offer better support to your nonmonogamous friends is to challenge some of that language when you hear it being used. In the same way that anti–sex work language is used to degrade and shame sex workers, stigmatizing and judgmental words used to condemn nonmonogamous relationships reinforce those same types of prejudices and make it harder to lose the stigma. It's hard to articulate just how painful it can be to hear these types of remarks, especially from so-called allies in sex-positive spaces. Calling people out on their outdated or loaded language regarding nonmonogamy can help create acceptance in our shared spaces. When we make these types of efforts to genuinely question how people talk and see one another, the changes are usually quite gradual, but they add up and are meaningful.

> Stigmatizing and judgmental words used to condemn nonmonogamous relationships reinforce those same types of prejudices.

When we have a better idea of how support for sex workers and nonmonogamous people works and overlaps, we can get a clearer picture of why these groups need to show greater solidarity with *each other*. I've made an effort throughout this book to show just how much these two groups have in common. To be judged and stigmatized for your life choices is never OK. We should feel reasonably upset that these judgments have actual and tangible impacts on our daily lives, from interactions with strangers to interactions with our social institutions. The fact of the matter is that sex workers and nonmonogamous people share so many elements of discrimination and stigma that there needs to be a more concerted effort to bring these groups together to show greater solidarity with one another.

But how do we go about actually achieving it? Easy. The way we have gone about asserting the importance of solidarity within these groups, individually, can be applied across the board so that sex workers can better understand what nonmonogamous people experience in their lives and vice versa. Nonmonogamous people can show their solidarity for sex workers by tapping into resources, like established literature, community organizations and activists, that could help them learn more about stigma and discrimination and use them as the basis for allyship. Becoming aware of the shared conditions of this kind of discrimination can help people have a better sense of how to actively support and show solidarity for sex workers. This kind of solidarity works best when everyone can find common ground with similar goals and hopes for how to support one another. Affirming the importance of allies, the leadership of sex worker movements and shared goals can empower all people who act in solidarity with one another.

There are any number of ways to show solidarity with sex workers. First and foremost, learning to be a good ally to sex workers goes a long way in showing that not only do you care, but you are willing to use your own power and resources to help sex workers. For example, healthcare professionals, academics, researchers and other people in positions of social power can have a great deal of influence as allies to sex workers. Allies who work in healthcare are able to help limit the kind of discrimination sex workers face in accessing healthcare options like primary care or therapy. Researchers and feminist

activists can also use
their power and ability
to marshall resources,
make space or help
provide a voice for sex
workers. Allies have an
important role in fighting oppression
and standing up for sex workers, who
experience all kinds of discrimination
on a daily basis. Allies can also use their
voices to support marginalized groups
at the intersections of discrimination
that sex workers experience, including
ableism, transphobia and addiction-
related discrimination.

Another important way to show
solidarity in supporting sex workers is
education. While tons of sex workers,
myself included, are open to discussing
the nature of our work and sharing our
experiences and expertise, it can become
tiring. I don't always want to be in the

position of having to educate every person who has a question or a need to satisfy their curiosity about sex work. So, educating yourself and becoming aware of the many resources that are available about sex worker rights and the discrimination faced by sex workers can go a long way in showing solidarity with us. By taking into account our voices and our experiences with sex work, loved ones and people who support us can become even more supportive allies. It's hard to understate the importance of education for becoming a great ally to sex workers.

Final Thoughts

The intention with this book was to give sex workers and nonmonogamous people a resource that would offer insights on the common ground between these two groups and how to navigate some of their shared challenges.

It'll feel profoundly rewarding for me if some of you can take away something positive and meaningful from these pages. I hope that having a new perspective on how to navigate questions

of stigma and intimacy in both sex
work and nonmonogamy have helped
you see some of these connections in
your lives and experiences. I hope the
discussion on sexual health also gave
you some perspective on prioritizing
risk management, whether you need to
do that in your personal relationships,
in the sex trade or both. And I hope that
some of you have been able to better
appreciate the importance of support
and allyship between sex workers and
nonmonogamous people. Knowing
that there are networks of people who
support you and groups of like-minded
folks who see you, appreciate you and
want you to thrive is such a liberating
feeling. Having the opportunity to
connect with people who want what's
best for me and my partners reminds
me of the importance of continuing
to build bridges with others and

seek community with those around me. Whether you're a sex worker, a nonmonogamous person or both, never stop living your life on your own terms.

Additional Reading

Blue, Effy. "How to be a Supportive Partner to a Sex Worker." *Curious Fox.* https://www.wearecuriousfoxes.com/read/how-to-be-a-supportive-partner-to-a-sex-worker

Brown, Ginny. "So You Want to Try Polyamory." *Everyday Feminism.* April 7, 2014. https://everydayfeminism.com/2014/04/so-you-want-to-try-polyamory/

Hardy, Janet, and Dossie Easton. *The Ethical Slut, Third Edition: A Practical Guide to Polyamory, Open Relationships, and Other Freedoms in Sex and Love.* New York: Ten Speed Press, 2017.

Valentine-Chase, Matt. "Sex Work, Stigma and Whorephobia." *Wellcome Collection.* May 11, 2020. https://wellcomecollection.org/articles/XrVSwxAAACQAbRUu

About the

MORE THAN TWO® ESSENTIALS SERIES

More Than Two Essentials is a series of books by Canadian authors on focused topics in nonmonogamy. It is curated by Eve Rickert, author of *More Than Two, Second Edition: Cultivating Nonmonogamous Relationships with Kindness and Integrity*.

Learn more at morethantwo.ca.

More from the

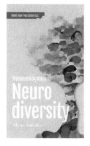

Nonmonogamy and Neurodiversity

Nonmonogamy and Death

Nonmonogamy and Happiness

Nonmonogamy and Teaching

Zara Shah is an Ontario-based writer. She has a BA in sociology and has worked in public relations. In 2008, she immigrated from Pakistan and uses writing as a tool to bridge the gap between Pakistani and Canadian culture and to highlight the immigrant experience.